Improve your sight-readi

CH00920061

Clarinet Grades 4–5

Paul Harris

NAME		

EXAMINATION RECORD

Grade	Date	Mark

TEACHER'S NAME
TELEPHONE

© 1994 by Faber Music Ltd
First published in 1994 by Faber Music Ltd
3 Queen Square London WC1N 3AU
Design and typography by James Butler
Music and text set by Silverfen
Cover illustration by Drew Hillier
Printed in England by Caligraving Ltd

ISBN 0-571-51465-0

INTRODUCTION

The ability to sight-read fluently is a most important part of your training as a clarinet player. Yet the *study* of sight-reading is often badly neglected by young players and is frequently regarded as no more than a rather unpleasant side-line. If you become a *good* sight-reader you will be able to learn pieces more quickly, and play in ensembles with confidence and assurance. Also, in grade examinations, good performance in the sight-reading test will result in useful extra marks!

Using the workbook

The purpose of this workbook is to incorporate sight-reading regularly into your practice and lessons, and to help you prepare for the sight-reading test in grade examinations. It offers you a progressive series of enjoyable and stimulating stages in which, with careful work, you should show considerable improvement from week to week.

Each stage consists of two parts: firstly, exercises which you should prepare in advance, along with a short piece with questions; and secondly, an unprepared test, to be found at the end of the book.

Your teacher will mark your work according to accuracy. Each stage carries a maximum of 50 marks and your work will be assessed as follows:

> 2 marks for each of the six questions relating to the prepared piece (total 12).
> 18 marks for the prepared piece itself.
> 20 marks for the unprepared test. (Teachers should devise a similar series of questions for the unprepared test, and take the answers into account when allocating a final mark.)

Space is given at the end of each stage for you to keep a running total of your marks as you progress. If you are scoring 40 or more each time you are doing well!

At the top of the first page in each stage you will see one or two new features to be introduced. There are then four different types of exercise:

1 **Rhythmic exercises** It is very important that you should be able to feel and maintain a steady beat. These exercises will help develop this ability. There are at least four ways of doing these exercises: clap or tap the lower line (the beat) while singing the upper line to 'la'; tap the lower line with your foot and clap the upper line; on a table or flat surface, tap the lower line with one hand and the upper line with the other; 'play' the lower line on a metronome and clap or tap the upper line.

2 **Melodic exercises** Fluent sight-reading depends on recognising melodic shapes at first glance. These shapes are often related to scales and arpeggios. Before you begin, always notice the *key-signature* and the notes affected by it, along with any accidentals.

3 **A prepared piece with questions** You should prepare carefully both the piece and the questions, which are to help you think about and understand the piece before you play it. Put your answers in the spaces provided.

4 **An unprepared piece** Finally, your teacher will give you an *unprepared* test to be read *at sight*. Make sure you have read the *Sight-reading Checklist* on page 21 before you begin each piece.

Remember to count throughout each piece and to keep going at a steady and even tempo. Always try to look ahead, at least to the next note or beat.

STAGE 1

RHYTHMIC EXERCISES

1

2

3

MELODIC EXERCISES

1

2

3

4

This music is copyright. Photocopying is illegal.

PREPARED PIECE

		Marks*
1	Explain the time-signature. What will you count?	2
2	What does *Allegro giocoso* mean?	1
3	In which key is this piece written?	2
4	What is the character of the music?	2
5	What do the dots above or below some of the notes indicate?	2
6	What do bars 1, 8 and 12 have in common?	2
	Total:	11

fast
lively   *playful*

Allegro giocoso

Unprepared tests page 22

Mark: ☐

Prepared work total: ☐

Unprepared: ☐

Total: ☐

*The mark boxes are to be filled in by your teacher (see Introduction).

STAGE 2

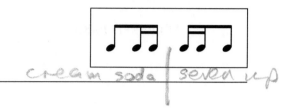

cream soda / seven up

RHYTHMIC EXERCISES

MELODIC EXERCISES

PREPARED PIECE

1   What does *Andante* mean?

2   In which key is this piece written?

3   What is the character of the music?

4   How often does the rhythm of bar 1 return?

5   How will you count bars 2 and 6 to ensure accuracy?

6   What does the symbol over the last note indicate?

Total:

Unprepared tests page 23   Mark:

Prepared work total:

Unprepared:

Total:

Running totals:

1   2

STAGE 3

A major

RHYTHMIC EXERCISES

MELODIC EXERCISES

PREPARED PIECE

15/12/09

1 In which key is the piece written? ☐

2 Mark the G sharps with a cross. ☐

3 What do the dots above or below some of the notes indicate? ☐

with motion

4 What does *Allegretto con moto* mean? ☐

5 What is the character of this piece? ☐

6 How will you make your performance musical? ☐

Total: ☐

Allegretto con moto

p cresc.

rall.

Unprepared tests page 24

Mark: ☐

Prepared work total: ☐

Unprepared: ☐

Total: ☐

Running totals:

1	2	3

STAGE 4

E minor $\frac{5}{4}$ $\frac{5}{8}$

RHYTHMIC EXERCISES

MELODIC EXERCISES

PREPARED PIECE

1 Explain the time-signature. What will you count?

2 What does *Con moto* mean?

3 In which key is this piece written?

4 Can you find an example of a full one octave scale?
  What form of the scale is used?

5 What is the character of this piece?

6 Clap the following rhythm:

Con moto

Unprepared tests page 25

Mark:

Prepared work total:

Unprepared:

Total:

Running totals:

1	2	3	4

STAGE 5

RHYTHMIC EXERCISES

1

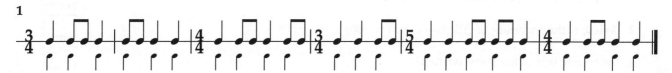

2

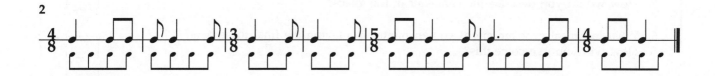

3

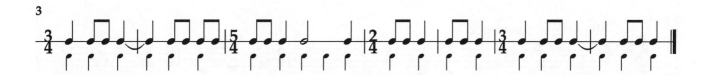

MELODIC EXERCISES

1

2

3

PREPARED PIECE

1 In which note values will you count this piece?

2 What is the meaning of *Allegro ma non troppo*?

3 In which key is the piece written?

4 What does the sign $\bar{p}$ indicate?

5 How would you describe the character of this piece?

6 What technical problem might you encounter in playing the final three bars? How will you overcome this?

Total:

Allegro ma non troppo

Unprepared tests page 26

Mark:

Prepared work total:

Unprepared:

Total:

Running totals:

1	2	3	4	5

STAGE 6

More rhythms in $\frac{6}{8}$

RHYTHMIC EXERCISES

MELODIC EXERCISES

14

PREPARED PIECE

1 Explain the time signature. How many beats will you count in each bar?

2 In which key is the piece written?

3 Mark with a cross any notes affected by the key signature.

4 For how many beats should the E (bars 7-8) be held?

5 What is the meaning of *rall. (rallentando)*?
　　　　　　　　　　cresc. (crescendo)?
　　　　　　　　　　dim. (diminuendo)?

6 What does *Andante sostenuto* mean?

Total:

Unprepared tests page 27　　　　　　　　Mark:

Prepared work total:

Unprepared:

Total:

Running totals:

1	2	3	4	5	6

STAGE 7

RHYTHMIC EXERCISES

MELODIC EXERCISES

PREPARED PIECE

1 In which key is this piece written?

2 How will you count this piece?

3 Where does the music of the first two bars return?

4 How do the two versions differ?

5 In what kind of music would you often find syncopation?

6 How many bars contain syncopated rhythms in this piece?

Total:

Unprepared tests page 28

Mark:

Prepared work total:

Unprepared:

Total:

Running totals:

1	2	3	4	5	6	7

STAGE 8

More rhythms in $\frac{6}{8}$
C minor

RHYTHMIC EXERCISES

MELODIC EXERCISES

PREPARED PIECE

1 In which key is this piece written?

2 Which form of the scale is used?

3 How would you describe the character of the music?

4 How will you count this piece?

5 Does the opening idea return – if so, does it differ?

6 What do the dots above or below some of the notes indicate?

Total:

Allegretto con moto

mf

cresc.

f

p

rall.

cresc.

mf

Unprepared tests page 29

Mark:

Prepared work total:

Unprepared:

Total:

Running totals:

1	2	3	4	5	6	7	8

STAGE 9

Eb major

RHYTHMIC EXERCISES

MELODIC EXERCISES

PREPARED PIECE

1 How will you count this piece? ☐

2 In which key is this piece written? ☐

3 What does the marking ♩ indicate? ☐

4 What do you notice about the dynamic levels in this piece? ☐

5 What does *Scherzando* mean? How will this influence your performance? ☐

6 What does *senza rit.* mean? ☐

Total: ☐

Unprepared tests page 30

Mark: ☐

Prepared work total: ☐

Unprepared: ☐

Total: ☐

Running totals:

1	2	3	4	5	6	7	8	9

CONCLUSION

A sight-reading checklist

Before you begin to play a piece at sight, always remember to consider the following:

1   Look at the key-signature, and find the notes which need raising or lowering.

2   Look at the time-signature, and decide how you will count the piece.

3   Notice any accidentals that may occur.

4   Notice scale and arpeggio patterns.

5   Work out leger-line notes if necessary.

6   Notice dynamic and other markings.

7   Look at the tempo mark and decide what speed to play.

8   Count one bar before you begin, to establish the speed.

When performing your sight-reading piece, always remember to:

1   CONTINUE TO COUNT THROUGHOUT THE PIECE.

2   Keep going at a steady and even tempo.

3   Ignore mistakes.

4   Check the key-signature at the beginning of each new line.

5   Look ahead – at least to the next beat or note.

6   Play *musically*.

UNPREPARED TESTS
STAGE 1

20/10/09

1 Andantino espressivo

2 Allegro moderato

3 Moderato cantabile

STAGE 2

1   Moderato

2   Andante

3   Allegretto scherzando

STAGE 3

STAGE 4

1   Andante espressivo

2   Con moto

3   Animato

STAGE 5

1   Con fuoco

2   Allegro ma non troppo

3   Allegro

STAGE 6

1   Lento espressivo

2   Andante con moto

3   Allegro moderato

STAGE 7

1 Lento

2 Rhumba - allegro moderato

3 Medium swing

STAGE 8

1   Allegro ritmico

2   Flowing

3   Allegro marcato

STAGE 9

Are you paralysed with fear
every time you go on stage?

Discover how to turn nerves
to your advantage.

3. If you are not a pianist, try and make sure you have as much practice with your accompanist as possible. It's important that you know the accompaniment as well. After all, it is part of the music! And don't be afraid of your accompanist. You are the soloist and they are there to make music with you. The same goes for ensemble playing. Getting to know your colleagues and how they may deal with nerves is as important as practising the notes.

Don't be afraid of your accompanist …

4. If you are playing several pieces in your recital and you are able to devise the programme order, it is often helpful to start with a piece you know well or a piece that isn't too technically demanding. This way you allow yourself the best warming-up conditions and are more likely to control your nerves.
5. Make sure you like the music you are playing. Enjoying what you do is another key element to reducing any nerves you may feel. It's your performance and you need to be in control.

8. Allow ... predict what ... contingency plan so that if you ... sitting around. See if there is a park or a café nearby where you could use any spare time you have doing something not connected with the impending performance. Above all, use the time to relax.

Allow plenty of time to get to the venue, as you can never predict what might happen en route …

12

13

Keeping your nerve! is the perfect prop for the young or amateur performer affected by stage fright. Full of comforting, easy-to-find advice and amusing anecdotes, this book will help you to:

· prepare for your performance, whether for a concert or exam
· enjoy performing, wherever and whenever
· unwind after the performance
· understand why you perform and why your audience turns up

Kate Jones also teams up with a star-studded cast of sympathetic performers and teachers, including Joanna MacGregor, Elvis Costello and Steven Isserlis, who reveal the special tactics that prevent them from turning to jelly!

"An invaluable, wonderful book. This must be in every musician's hands, young or old!"
(*Evelyn Glennie*)

Keeping your nerve!   ISBN 0-571-51922-9

Welcome to …

Paul Harris's
Clarinet Basics

Clarinet Basics is a landmark method by one of the leading figures in clarinet education. It starts at absolute beginner level and progresses to about Grade 2 level. The method is set out in 22 stages, each of which includes:

- a wonderful variety of concert pieces from the great composers

- traditional tunes and fun, original exercises

- 'finger gyms' and 'warm ups' to help establish a sound technique

- invaluable 'fact files' and 'quizzes' to teach notation and general musicianship

- helpful, clear 'fingering charts' and 'rhythm boxes'

- great illustrations!

The separate teacher's book contains clarinet and piano accompaniments, suggestions for group work and teaching tips.

Clarinet Basics (pupil's book) ISBN 0-571-51814-1
Clarinet Basics (teacher's book) ISBN 0-571-51815-X
Clarinet Basics (accompaniment CD) ISBN 0-571-52167-3